Math
Road Trip

An Interactive Discovery-Based Math Unit for High-Ability Learners

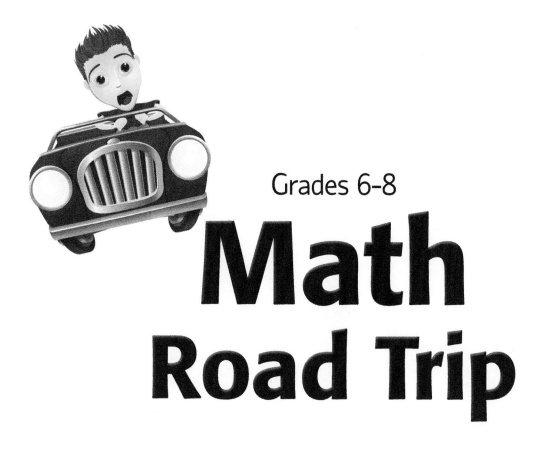

Grades 6-8

Math
Road Trip

Richard G. Cote & Darcy O. Blauvelt

 Routledge
Taylor & Francis Group

NEW YORK AND LONDON

First published in 2013 by Prufrock Press Inc.

Published in 2021 by Routledge
605 Third Avenue, New York, NY 10017
2 Park Square, Milton Park, Abingdon, Oxon OX14 4RN

Routledge is an imprint of the Taylor & Francis Group, an informa business

Copyright © 2013 by Taylor & Francis Group

Production design by Raquel Trevino

ISBN: 9781032141503 (hbk)
ISBN: 9781618210463 (pbk)

DOI: 10.4324/9781003236511

Table of Contents

Introduction

Background

Gifted program directors, resource specialists, and—perhaps most importantly—general education classroom teachers who struggle with the challenge of providing appropriate services to students of high potential in the traditional classroom will be interested in these Interactive Discovery-Based Units for High-Ability Learners. The units encourage students to use nontraditional methods to demonstrate learning.

Any given curriculum is composed of two distinct, though not separate, entities: content and context. In every classroom environment, there are forces at work that define the content to be taught. These forces may take the form of high-stakes tests or local standards. But in these Interactive Discovery-Based Units for High-Ability Learners, the context of a traditional classroom is reconfigured so that students are provided with a platform from which to demonstrate academic performance and understanding that are not shown through traditional paper-and-pencil methods. This way, teachers go home smiling and students go home tired at the end of the school day.

C = C + C
Curriculum = Content + Context

In March of 2005, the Further Steps Forward Project (FSFP) was established and funded under the Jacob K. Javits Gifted and Talented Students Education Program legislation. The project had a two-fold, long-range mission:

- The first goal was to identify, develop, and test identification instruments specific to special populations of the gifted, focusing on the economically disadvantaged.
- The second goal was to create, deliver, and promote professional development focused on minority and underserved populations of the gifted, especially the economically disadvantaged.

The result was the Student Context Rubric (SCR), which is included in each of the series' eight units. The SCR, discussed in further depth in the Appendix, is a rubric that a teacher or specialist uses to evaluate a student in five areas: engagement, creativity, synthesis, interpersonal ability, and verbal communication. When used in conjunction with the units in this series, the SCR provides specialists with an excellent tool for identifying students of masked potential—students who are gifted but are not usually recognized—and it gives general education teachers the language necessary to advocate for these students when making recommendations for gifted and additional services. The SCR also provides any teacher with a tool for monitoring and better understanding student behaviors.

Using best practices from the field of gifted education as a backdrop, we viewed students through the lens of the following core beliefs as we developed each unit:

- instrumentation must be flexible in order to recognize a variety of potentials;
- curricula must exist that benefit all students while also making clear which students would benefit from additional services; and
- identification processes and services provided by gifted programming must be integral to the existing curriculum; general education teachers cannot view interventions and advocacy as optional.

These eight contextually grounded units, two in each of the four core content areas (language arts, social studies, math, and science), were developed to serve as platforms from which middle school students could strut their stuff, displaying their knowledge and learning in practical, fun contexts. Four of the units (*Ecopolis, Mathematics in the Marketplace, Order in the Court,* and *What's Your Opinion?*) have been awarded the prestigious National Association for Gifted Children (NAGC) Curriculum Award. Over the span of 3 years, we—and other general education teachers—taught all of the units multiple times to measure their effectiveness as educational vehicles and to facilitate dynamic professional development experiences.

The FSFP documented that in 11 of 12 cases piloted in the 2008–2009 school year, middle school students showed statistically significant academic gains. In particular, those students who were underperforming in the classroom showed great progress. Furthermore, there were statistically significant improvements in students' perceptions of their classroom environments in terms of innovation and involvement. Finally, the contextually grounded units in this series can be used as springboards for further study and projects, offering teachers opportunities for cross-disciplinary collaboration.

Administrators, teachers, and gifted specialists will gain from this series a better sense of how to develop and use contextualized units—not only in the regular education classroom, but also in gifted programming.

How to Use the Units

Every lesson in the units includes an introductory section listing the concepts covered, suggested materials, grade-level expectations, and student objectives. This section also explains how the lesson is introduced, how students demonstrate recognition of the concepts, how they apply their knowledge, and how they solve related problems. The lesson plans provided, while thorough, also allow for differentiation and adaptation. Depending on how much introduction and review of the material students need, you may find that some lessons take more or less time than described. We have used these units in 50-minute class periods, but the subparts of the lesson—introducing the material, recognizing the concepts, applying knowledge, and solving a problem—allow for adaptability in terms of scheduling. The "Additional Notes" for each lesson provide further tips, flag potential problem areas, and offer suggestions for extending the lesson.

This series offers many contextual units from which to choose; however, we do not recommend using them exclusively. In our research, we have found that students who are constantly involved in contextual learning become immune to its benefits. We recommend, therefore, that you vary the delivery style of material across the school year. For most classes, spacing out three contextual units over the course of the year produces optimal results.

These units may be used in place of other curricula. However, if you find that your students are stumbling over a specific skill as they progress through a unit, do not hesitate to take a day off from the unit and instead use direct instruction to teach that skill. (For instance, in this unit, you may pause the unit for some direct instruction regarding the scientific method.) This will help to ensure that students are successful as they move forward. It is necessary for students to be frustrated and challenged, as this frustration serves as the impetus of learning—yet they must not be so frustrated that they give up. Throughout the unit, you must find the delicate balance between providing challenges for your students and overwhelming them.

The Role of the Teacher

A contextual unit is a useful vehicle both for engaging your students and for assessing their abilities. As a teacher, your role changes in a contextual unit. Rather than being the driving force, you are the behind-the-scenes producer. The students are the drivers of this creative vehicle. If you are used to direct instruction methods of teaching, you will need to make a conscious choice not to run the show. Although this may feel a bit uncomfortable for you in the beginning, the rewards for your students will prove well worth the effort. As you become more comfortable with the process, you will find that this teaching method is conducive to heightening student engagement and learning while also allowing you to step back and observe your students at work.

Group Dynamics

Cooperation plays a key role in this unit. Small-group work is fraught with challenges for all of us. Creating groups that will be able to accomplish their objectives—groups whose members will fulfill their roles—takes some forethought. Keep in mind that sometimes the very act of working through any issues that arise may be the most powerful learning tool of all. Before beginning the unit, you should discuss with students the importance of working together and assigning tasks to ensure that work is distributed and completed fairly and equally.

Preparation and Pacing

Deciding on a timeline is very important as you plan the implementation of the unit. You know your students better than anyone else does. Some students may be more successful when they are immersed in the unit, running it every day for 3 weeks. Others would benefit from having some days off to get the most out of their experiences.

Every classroom is different. Students possess different sets of prior knowledge, learning strategies, and patterns. This means that as the teacher, you must make decisions about how much of the material you will introduce prior to the unit, whether you will provide occasional traditional instruction throughout the unit, how many days off you will give students, and how much your students will discover on their own throughout the course of the unit. For example, in this science unit, students perform a series of experiments to experience the differences between physical and chemical changes. You may choose to teach these concepts prior to using the unit, and then use the unit to replace the practice days that would usually follow. Another option is to use the unit without preteaching these concepts, instead allowing the unit's activities to show which students already possess some content knowledge and which students are experiencing more difficulty. If you choose the latter option, it is important to use the pretest carefully and to cultivate an encouraging atmosphere in the classroom. The pretest is somewhat unconventional, as students are prompted simply to write everything that they know about physical and chemical changes. This intentional open-ended preassessment allows students a wider than usual opportunity to demonstrate any levels of scientific thinking (observe, organize, infer, and predict) they may possess at the outset of the unit. The optional lesson covers this type of scientific thinking in more depth. As an end-of-unit assessment, students will be asked to generate visual aids and develop a presentation in addition to writing. This book is not meant to provide exact instructions; in every lesson, there is wiggle room in terms of how you work alongside students to enable them to demonstrate learning.

Also, you should feel free to use materials other than those suggested. If there is a topic or source that is highly relevant for your students, then it might be worthwhile for you to compile research sites, articles, and other materials about the topic in order to provide your students a degree of real-world involvement.

Using these units is a bit like using a recipe in the kitchen. The first time you use one of the units, you may want to use it just as it is written. Each successive time you use it, however, you may choose to adjust the ratios and substitute ingredients to suit your own tastes. The more you personalize the units to your students' situations and preferences, the more engaged they will be—and the same goes for you as the teacher.

Common Core State Standards

The Common Core State Standards, as well as the Smarter Balance tests, focus on synthesis as a representation of depth of knowledge. Synthesis of information is a hallmark of these discovery-based interactive units. In each interactive unit, the lessons have been aligned with the Common Core State Standards to better illustrate the focus of the activities. Research has shown that the use of the authentic performance assessments provided in each of the discovery-based units in the series promotes greater depth and breadth of understanding of content, which is a major thrust of these nationally developed standards.

Adaptability

"Organized chaos" is a phrase often used to describe a contextual classroom. The students are not sitting at their desks and quietly taking notes while the teacher delivers information verbally. A classroom full of students actively engaged in their learning and creatively solving real-world problems is messy, but highly productive. Every teacher has his or her own level of tolerance for this type of chaos, and you may find yourself needing days off occasionally. Organization is an essential ingredient for success in a contextual unit. For example, you will need a place in your classroom where students can access paperwork. It is important to think through timeframes and allow for regular debriefing sessions.

You will also want to develop a personalized method for keeping track of who is doing what. Some students will be engaged from the start, but others you will need to prod and encourage to become involved. This will be especially true if your students are unfamiliar with this type of contextual learning. There are always a few students who try to become invisible so that classmates will do their work for them. Others may be Tom Sawyers, demonstrating their interpersonal skills by persuading peers to complete their work. You will want to keep tabs on both of these types of students so that you can maximize individual student learning. Some teachers have students keep journals, others use daily exit card strategies, and others use checklists. Again, many aspects of how to use these units are up to you.

It is difficult in a busy classroom to collect detailed behavioral data about your students, but one advantage of contextual learning is that it is much easier to spend observation time in the classroom when you are not directly running the show! If you have the luxury of having an assistant or classroom visitor who can help you collect anecdotal data, then we recommend keeping some sort of log of student behavior. What has worked well for us has been to create a list of students' pictures, with a blank box next to each picture in which behaviors can be recorded.

Contextual units require the teacher to do a considerable amount of work prior to beginning the unit, but once you have put everything into place, the students take over and you can step back and observe as they work, solve problems, and learn.

Unit Overview

This unit is designed to assess the degree to which students understand and can apply basic mathematics concepts, including the four basic operations applied to fractions and decimals, distance = rate × time, ratio and proportion, and scale drawing. Participation will test students' abilities regardless of the role to which they are assigned. For example, a highly able student will have the opportunity to excel as a leader, navigator, or mathematician/cartographer. Assigning student roles is as much a function of their maturity, temperament, and spirit of cooperation as it is a matter of ability.

Students are given the opportunity to develop effective planning and budgeting skills. They will learn to read maps, determine distances traveled, draw a map to scale, and organize information. Opportunities are also provided for students to sharpen public speaking and presentation skills. *Math Road Trip* can easily be modified to include an emphasis on geography if that is so desired.

Each lesson is structured to include the following elements: introduction, recognition, application, and problem solving. The concept of the lesson is *introduced* by the teacher. The students are given the opportunity to show that they *recognize* the concept. They are provided the opportunity to *apply* the concept, and are challenged to *solve a problem* using the concept. By organizing each lesson into these four divisions the teacher has more latitude in differentiating the lesson based on student prior knowledge, skills, level of engagement, and readiness. It is left to the teacher to determine where to start each student.

Unit Outline

We designed these lessons to be used during 50-minute class periods. Depending on the extent to which you need to review concepts with your students and the amount of time you decide to devote to particular activities, some of these lessons may take fewer or more days than indicated. We have tried to note how many days each lesson will take to complete.

Lesson 1

Students complete the Math Skills Delineator (pretest) and are assigned to teams. Each team plans a postgame party. (*Note*: This lesson requires 2 days.)

Lesson 2

Students are given the opportunity to plan trips to destinations that are of increasing distance from home. The lesson culminates with students planning a trip to an international destination and addresses the difficulties that international travel brings. (*Note*: This lesson requires 2 days.)

Lesson 3

Students develop a set of directions that will be used to guide a team of their classmates from a starting point to an end point.

Lesson 4

Students explore the concepts of ratio and proportion by constructing a treasure map that is drawn to scale. (*Note*: This lesson requires 2 days.)

Lesson 5

Team building is stressed, as students must reach consensus with respect to all of the materials needed for the *Math Road Trip*.

Lesson 6

Students receive an appropriate *Math Road Trip* prompt and a hypothetical family for whom they are to plan a vacation. On the third day of this lesson, class presentations are made and a *Math Road Trip* rubric (performance measure) is completed by the teacher. Students, meanwhile, listen to presentations and take notes, to be used as constructive feedback for presenters. (*Note*: This lesson requires 3 days.)

Lesson 7

Students provide constructive criticism of the *Math Road Trip* unit by responding to the issues raised on the evaluation sheet provided. Students also evaluate their personal performance while participating in *Math Road Trip* and take the Math Skills Delineator as a posttest to determine gains in content knowledge.

Glossary of Terms

For the purposes of this unit, the following definitions will be used.

- **Budget:** The amount of money that will be spent for various purposes in a given amount of time.
- **Cartographer:** The maker of maps or charts.
- **Compass Rose:** An instrument used for showing directions.
- **Consensus:** A general agreement reached by all the participants.
- **Hypothetical:** Based on something that is assumed.
- **Itinerary:** Details of a trip or schedule that is planned.
- **Legend:** The explanation of the symbols used on a map or diagram.
- **Map:** A drawing or chart showing the distance and direction between towns, cities, rivers, lakes, and other physical features found on Earth.
- **Meter:** The basic unit of length used in the metric system of measurement.
- **Navigator:** The person in charge of determining the distance and direction between two towns, cities, rivers, lakes, or other physical features found on Earth.
- **Rate:** The change in distance per unit time.
- **Scale:** The size of a plan, map, drawing, or model compared with what it actually represents.

Lesson 1

Concepts

- Addition of decimals
- Reading a street map
- Developing an itinerary

Materials

- Math Skills Delineator (p. 15; answer key on p. 17)
- Math Skills Delineator Answer Sheet (p. 16)
- Group Roles sheet (p. 18)
- Planning Challenge 1 sheet (p. 19)
- Food and Beverage Options sheet (p. 21)
- Local street/road maps

Student Objective

Students demonstrate an ability to read a street map and to add decimals by determining a route to follow and a list of foods to acquire to plan a postgame party.

Introduction

After taking the Math Skills Delineator, students are assigned to work in groups of three to complete Planning Challenge 1: A Day in _____.

DOI: 10.4324/9781003236511-1

Recognition

Students acknowledge that they must plan a postgame party by staying within a $38 budget.

Application

The teacher distributes the Group Roles sheet, the Food and Beverage Options sheet, and the Planning Challenge 1 sheet. Students then work in groups to complete Planning Challenge 1.

Problem Solving

Students should evaluate their work by writing a paragraph on the most challenging part of the day.

Common Core State Standards Met

- CCSS-Math: 6.NS.A Apply and extend previous understandings of multiplication and division to divide fractions by fractions.
- CCSS-Math: 6.NS.C Apply and extend previous understandings of numbers to the system of rational numbers.
- CCSS-Math: 6.RP.A Understand ratio concepts and use ratio reasoning to solve problems.
- CCSS-Math: 7.NS.A Apply and extend previous understandings of operations with fractions.

Additional Notes

- Use the Math Skills Delineator to establish a baseline of students' math skills. Please make students aware that this exercise is not for grading purposes, but rather to help you determine the role each student will play in his or her assigned group.
- We have left the name of the town/city in the title of the Planning Challenge 1 worksheet blank to allow you to substitute the name of your location. We have found it more beneficial for students to begin with a location with which they are familiar. Blank spaces have also been provided throughout the exercise to enable you to customize the activity to your own location.
- The teacher should assign students to groups. The students may make recommendations as to which role they wish to play. The teacher, however, makes the final assignments.

- Please note that it is suggested that teachers take 2 days to accomplish this lesson. We have found success with administering the Math Skills Delineator and the Group Roles sheet on Day 1 and using Day 2 to complete Planning Challenge 1. The final decision with respect to pacing is left to the discretion of the teacher.

Math Skills Delineator

1. 7.64
    + 4.1

2. 8.43
    + 4.162

3. 2.601
    + .015

4. 5.064 + 7.2

5. 3.61 + 2.5 + 14.7

6. 14.6
    − 5.82

7. (14.3)(6.8)

8. (9.05)(.3)

9. 712.48 ÷ 5.84

10. 3.738 ÷ 2.1

11. John takes a long bicycle ride. He travels 10.8 miles to visit his friend Mary. The trip takes him 2.3 hours. How fast (rate) was John going?

12. Fred jogs at a rate of 2.5 meters/second. How many minutes does it take for him to run 3,000 meters? (Reminder: There are 60 seconds in one minute.)

13. If 2 cups of butter are used to bake 8 dozen cookies, how much butter will be needed to bake 12 dozen cookies?

14. On a map, ½ inch represents a distance of 20 miles in real life. The distance between two towns is 3 ½ inches on the map. How far apart are the two towns in real life?

Math Skills Delineator

Answer Sheet

1. _____   8. _____

2. _____   9. _____

3. _____   10. _____

4. _____   11. _____

5. _____   12. _____

6. _____   13. _____

7. _____   14. _____

Math Skills Delineator

Answer Key

1. 11.74
2. 12.592
3. 2.616
4. 12.264
5. 20.81
6. 8.78
7. 97.24

8. 2.715
9. 122
10. 1.78
11. 4.7 mi/hr
12. 20 minutes
13. 3 cups
14. 140 miles

Group Roles

In this lesson you will need the following roles within your group. Please read the job descriptions carefully and make your recommendations based on team members' strengths. The teacher will make the final assignments.

- **Leader:** This person must be a good negotiator and must be focused and able to encourage others in a positive way. This person is responsible for keeping costs within the budget. The leader is also responsible for providing updates to the teacher when asked. Ultimately, it is the leader's responsibility that the group is successful.
- **Navigator:** This person needs to follow directions, have an attention for detail, and be able to listen to others' suggestions. The navigator is responsible for reading maps and for developing a legend of local landmarks, rivers, lakes, rail lines, and other features when the team creates maps of its own.
- **Cartographer:** The cartographer's job is to create a map of the route that needs to be taken to achieve the group's goal. The map will include landmarks from the legend developed by the navigator.

Leader: _____

Navigator: _____

Cartographer: _____

Please note that this is a group project; therefore, everyone can help in any area, but it is the responsibility of each individual to see that his or her job is complete.

Planning Challenge 1

A Day in _____

Today is the championship game for _____!
You live on the corner of _____ and

_____Streets, in historic

_____.You have invited 8 friends over for a party,

to take place after the 1 p.m. game. The food budget for the party is $38. You're

too young to drive, therefore you do not have a car to use for your errands for the

party.

Plot the most direct walking route to take you to the following places:

- A bakery on _____ Street
- A fruit stand on _____ Street
- A grocery store on _____ Street

Don't forget that you must get all of the food home and get to the stadium by 1
p.m. for the ceremonial first pitch!

Itinerary:

We will leave the house at _____.

We will do our errands in the following order:

1. _____

2. _____

3. _____

4. _____

We will arrive home by _____ .

We will leave for the stadium at _____ .

Our menu for the party will be:

The total cost will be _____ .

Please show how the total cost of the postgame party was determined.

Food and Beverage Options

Bakery	Estimated Cost
Cakes	$19.95 each
Pies	$15 each
A dozen cookies	$6.50
A dozen bread rolls	$4.25

Fruit Stand	Estimated Cost
A dozen oranges	$3.75
A dozen apples	$2.79
A bunch of bananas (6)	$2.85
Watermelon	$0.45/lb

Grocery Store	Estimated Cost
A case of soda	$5.65
A gallon of fruit juice	$2.49
A bag of chips	$1.79
A bag of pretzels	$1.49
A pound of cheese	$4.39
A box of crackers	$2.28

Lesson 2

Concepts

- Mileage
- Cost of automobile transportation
- Planning a trip
- Staying within a budget

Materials

- Transportation Costs sheet (p. 25; answer key on p. 27)
- Expense Log sheet (p. 28)
- Itinerary sheet (p. 31)
- Planning Challenge 2–5 sheets (pp. 32–35)
- Local, state, national, and international maps

Note: Providing students with Internet access will greatly facilitate your efforts.

Student Objective

Students demonstrate the ability to plan a trip and to stay within budget by submitting an expense log and an itinerary sheet for hypothetical travel to (a) a nearby city, (b) New York City, and (c) Washington, DC. An international trip to Montreal culminates the lesson.

Introduction

Students are reminded of their roles by revisiting the Group Roles sheet they completed in Lesson 1. Groups should evaluate their work in Planning Challenge

DOI: 10.4324/9781003236511-2

1. Was each group member able to do his or her part in meeting the challenge? Do they want to renegotiate their roles? You may choose to reassign roles based on student performances in Lesson 1 at your discretion. Students should also choose team names for their groups at this time.

Recognition

Students complete the Transportation Costs sheet.

Application

Students complete an Expense Log and Itinerary for one of the three domestic trips described in Planning Challenge 2, Planning Challenge 3, or Planning Challenge 4.

Problem Solving

Students plan an international visit to Montreal (Planning Challenge 5) to recover hidden treasure.

Common Core State Standards Met

- CCSS-Math: 6.RP.A Understand ratio concepts and use ratio reasoning to solve problems.
- CCSS-Math: 7.RP.A Analyze proportional relationships and use them to solve real-world and mathematical problems.

Additional Notes

- Lesson 1 can be used to affirm the decisions that were made in group assignments as well as the role assignments. It is important for the teacher to act on their observations and reassign groups and/or roles as necessary.
- The Transportation Costs sheet that students work on at the outset of this lesson will provide you with an additional opportunity to judge which groups are working well together and which may be dysfunctional.
- Depending upon your location (the distance you are from a nearby city; New York City; Washington, DC; and Montreal) and local conditions, you may choose to change the amount that has been budgeted for each trip.
- Gasoline prices are volatile, therefore you may choose to adjust them dependent on prices in your region at the time the lesson is implemented. The

problems on the Transportation Costs sheet and the Expense Log are only designed to help you determine students' skill levels.

- As mentioned in the note to the teacher (see the Materials section earlier in the lesson), it's much more efficient to allow students to use the Internet to access local, state, national, and international maps. Otherwise, you might find yourself scrambling to acquire these maps. If no access is possible, AAA is usually a good source as they give away many maps as they update their existing supplies.

Transportation Costs

Example:

John drives 45 miles round trip to work each day. His car gets 25 miles per gallon. If gasoline costs $3.68 per gallon, how much does it cost John to go to (and return) from work each day? (Round to the nearest cent.)

Solution:

A. $\begin{array}{r} 45 \text{ miles} \\ \times\ 2 \text{ round trips} \\ \hline 90 \text{ miles each day} \end{array}$

B. 90 miles ÷ 25 miles = gal used

$$\begin{array}{r} 3.6 \\ 25\overline{\smash{)}90.0} \\ -75.0 \\ \hline 15.0 \\ -15\,0 \\ \hline 0 \end{array}$$

C. 3.6 gal at $3.68/gal

$$\begin{array}{r} 3.68 \\ \times\ 3.6 \\ \hline 2208 \\ +1104 \\ \hline 13.248 \end{array}$$

It costs John $13.25 to drive to work each day.

Now, determine the costs for the following driving situations. Round your answers to the nearest hundredth place.

1.   78 miles driven; 20 miles/gal; gas costs $3.50/gal

_____

2.   300 miles driven; 25 miles/gal; gas costs $3.65/gal

_____

3.   460 miles driven; 18 miles/gal; gas costs $3.78/gal

_____

4.   1,360.2 miles driven; 21.5 miles/gal; gas costs $3.60/gal

_____

5.   368.4 miles driven; 23.2 miles/gal; gas costs $3.47/gal

_____

Math Road Trip © Taylor & Francis Group

Transportation Costs

Answer Key

1. $13.65
2. $43.80
3. $96.60
4. $227.75
5. $55.10

Name: _____

Team: _____

Date: _____

Expense Log

Destination: _____

Day	Transportation	Meals	Lodging	Activity	Other	Total
1						
2						
3						
4						
Total						

Transportation

➤ Total miles driven _____ / 30 miles per gallon = _____ × 3.68

= cost of driving: _____

➤ Total miles walked _____ × 0 = cost of walking: _____

➤ Other fares (e.g., train, airplane, bus, taxi): _____

➤ Cost of driving_____ + cost of walking _____ +

other fares _____ = cost of transportation:_____

Meals

Number of people _____ × number of meals each _____ × price

per meal _____ = cost of meals: _____

(*Note:* Using this formula, costs for breakfast, lunch, and dinner should be calculated separately and then totaled. Other formulas are also possible. See the Itinerary sheet for meal costs.)

Breakfast:_____

Lunch: _____

Dinner: _____

Total: _____

Lodging

Number of people _____ × number of nights _____ × $65 =

cost of lodging: _____

Activities

➢ Museums: $15 per person
➢ Sports events: $12.75 per person (local teams) or $85 per person (professional teams)
➢ Movies: $12.35 per person

Tickets purchased _____ × price per ticket _____ =

cost of activity: _____

(*Note:* Using this formula, costs for each activity should be calculated separately and then totaled. Other formulas are also possible.)

Museums: _____

Sports events (local): _____

Sports events (professional): _____

Movies: _____

Total: _____

Cost of transportation _____ + cost of meals _____ + cost of lodging _____ + cost of activities _____ = total cost of trip:

_____

Name:_____ Date: _____

Team: _____

Itinerary

Destination: _____

Meals

	Breakfast	Lunch	Dinner	Total
Price Per Meal	$5.25	$10.35	$21.40	
Number of Meals				
Total				

Lodging

	Night 1	Night 2	Night 3	Total
Price Per Person	$65.00	$65.00	$65.00	
Number of People				
Total				

Activities

	Museum	Sports Event: Local	Sports Event: Pro	Movies	Total
Price Per Ticket	$15.00	$12.75	$85.00	$12.35	
Tickets Purchased					
Total					

Planning Challenge 2

Congratulations! Your group has been given a gift of $1,000 to be used for a trip to _____. While in this historic city, you are encouraged to experience as many cultural offerings as possible. Be sure to plan events for all of the members of your group. Here are some options you may want to consider:

- Will you spend the money to stay in the city, or will you drive back home each day? Map out your route and calculate all necessary transportation costs.
- How many meals will you need to plan for?
- While in the city, will you walk from place to place or take some form of public transportation (e.g., bus, taxi)? If you use public transportation, don't forget to determine the cost!

Be sure to fill out an Expense Log and Itinerary sheet when you are finished planning.

New York City

You are sitting in your cozy living room, enjoying a good movie, when your phone rings. It's the security chief of the Metropolitan Museum of Art in New York City. He is frantic! Someone has broken into the museum and stolen a rare artifact. The night watchman was shot trying to stop the thieves. It is hoped that he will survive, but the doctors are not optimistic. The security chief asks you to assemble your team and come to New York City as quickly as possible. He promises to pay all of your expenses up to $1,000 if you will help him.

You gather your team and set out for the Big Apple. Once you arrive in New York you go directly to the museum. As you investigate the crime scene you learn that the guard is waking up at the medical center on 5th Ave. The team hurries to his bedside. The guard tells you that the only thing he remembers is that one of the robbers was wearing a Hunter College sweatshirt. Your first major clue!

How many days will you have to solve the crime? Map out your route to New York and your travels within the city. You will be staying at a hotel on the corner of W 89th St. and Columbus Ave. Remember, in order to get paid you must fill out an Expense Log and an Itinerary sheet completely.

Happy hunting!

WASHINGTON, DC

Congratulations! You have won an all-expense-paid trip to Washington, DC. You have been given $1,000 to provide you and your team transportation to the city and hotel accommodations at the Hyatt Regency Hotel on Capitol Hill. How you spend the rest of your money is up to you, but in order to be reimbursed you must submit an Expense Log and Itinerary sheet at the end of your stay. Here are some things you may want to consider:

- How many nights will you stay?
- Remember that for every day that you are there, you must allow three meals per day per person.
- In addition to rooms and meals, you must plan an entertainment schedule that appeals to all of your team. One of you is fascinated by police work, another is a farmer, and the third is a train fanatic.

Good luck!

MONTREAL

Yesterday, a mysterious letter arrived in your mailbox. It instructed you to go to the city of Montreal as soon as possible. Once you arrive there you must find the Parc Charleroi on the Rue De Castille and Rue Louis Francoeur. In the center of the park is a large apple tree. Hidden in the trunk of the tree is a treasure that was stashed there for you and your family by a long-lost relative. The only thing you know is that the treasure is not cash.

You must be back within 3 days because of your work schedule. How will you retrieve your treasure and stay within a budget of $1,000? Will you have time and money for any other activities while in Montreal?

- How will you get there (e.g., plane, train, car)?
- What will be your total cost?
- What will you do if you have spare time?

You may develop your own forms to report the cost of the 3-day trip, or you may use the Expense Log and Itinerary sheet provided. Then, write a paragraph describing your favorite area of the city.

Lesson 3

Concepts

- Following directions
- Distance = speed × time

Materials

- Road maps (not provided)
- Direction Codes sheet (p. 38; answer key on p. 41)
- Giving Directions sheet (p. 42)

Student Objective

Students demonstrate the ability to arrive at a predetermined destination by following a set of directions developed by their classmates.

Introduction

The teacher underscores the importance of following directions and discusses the use of the compass rose that is provided on the Direction Codes worksheet.

Recognition

Working individually, students complete the Directions Codes worksheet.

DOI: 10.4324/9781003236511-3

Application

Students are to complete the Giving Directions sheet. Given a starting point, students (working in their groups of 3) are to write very clear directions that will enable another team to get to a destination determined by the writers. The journey must have a minimum of four legs, and each leg must contain a minimum of one landmark or map feature. Only speed and time are given. For example, one leg of the directions could be, *Start at the Manchester, NH, airport and proceed NE at 30 mi/hr for 30 minutes.*

Problem Solving

Students pass along the directions they have authored to another team whose task it is to arrive at the destination known only to the writing team.

Common Core State Standards Met

- CCSS-Math: 6.RP.A Understand ratio concepts and use ratio reasoning to solve problems.
- CCSS-Math: 6.SP.B Summarize and describe distributions.

Additional Notes

- Once again, the teacher can save time and effort by allowing students the use of the Internet rather than having to make several maps available.
- Inform students where the direction "north" is with respect to the classroom orientation.
- As an additional exercise using the compass rose, consider having one student give another student directions to navigate around an object in the classroom. To accomplish this task successfully, students will have to learn that the compass must remain aligned to north regardless of the turns they will make.

Direction Codes

Compass directions are used in helping people to navigate through land, sea, or air. In this activity, we are going to help create a code that explains the directions we are given. Refer to the compass rose on the right for the proper compass directions.

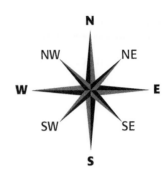

Let's take a look at an example of how to write a direction code. Look at the directions presented visually below.

The direction code would be written as follows: **N–NE–SE–S–SW–E**

Now, try your hand at the direction problems below. Remember to start at the dot and then follow the arrows.

1.

Code:_____

2.

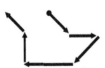

Code:_____

3.

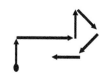

Code: _____

4.

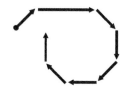

Code: _____

5.

Code:_____

6. In problems 2–5, what single direction would take you directly from the start to the finish? (For example, Problem 1 would be SE.)

2._____   3._____   4._____   5._____

7. You are in a car that is headed south. It you turn left, left, and then right (assume all turns are 90°), in what direction are you headed?

Direction: _____

8. You are headed west. You turn right, drive a mile, turn left, drive 3 miles, and then turn right for another mile. In what direction are you headed?

   Direction: _____

9. You are going southeast. After two left turns and one right turn, what direction are you going?

   Direction: _____

10. You are headed northwest. If you turn 90° to the right, 45° to the left, and finally turn 180° in the opposite direction, what direction are you headed?

    Direction: _____

Direction Codes

Answer Key

1. N–NE–SE–S–E–SW
2. SE–E–SW–W–N–NW
3. N–E–N–SE–SW–W
4. NE–E–SE–S–SW–W–NW–N
5. E–NE–E–SE–SW–N–SW
6. 2: W, 3: NE, 4: SE/E, 5: SE
7. E
8. N
9. NE
10. S

Name:_____ Date: _____

Giving Directions

Determine a final destination. Then, working from your given starting point, determine the directions necessary to guide others to your end location. Your journey must contain at least four legs, and each leg must include either a landmark or map feature. Include only speed and time in your directions.

Example: *Start at the Manchester-Boston Regional Airport in Manchester, NH, and proceed NE at 30mi/hr for 30 minutes.*

Landmark	Map Feature (e.g., rivers, mountains)
Leg 1	
Leg 2	
Leg 3	
Leg 4	
Leg 5	
Leg 6	

Lesson 4

Concepts

- Measurement
- Ratio and proportion
- Scale drawing

Materials

- Rulers and/or tape measures
- Introduction to Scale Drawing sheet (p. 46)
- Scale Drawing Practice sheet (p. 47; answer key on p. 48)
- Mystery Location Map sheet (p. 49)
- Directions sheet (p. 50)
- Discoveries sheet (p. 51)
- Personal Reflection sheet (p. 53)

Student Objective

Students demonstrate the ability to use a ruler and apply the concept of scale by constructing a map and directions that classmates use to find the mystery location.

Introduction

After students have received instruction in solving ratio and proportion problems (resource exercises provided), they experience using scale drawing to prepare for map reading.

DOI: 10.4324/9781003236511-4

Recognition

Students continue to work in assigned teams consisting of a leader, navigator, and cartographer. They review and study the Introduction to Scale Drawing sheet and complete the Scale Drawing Practice sheet.

Application

1. Students construct a map, drawn to scale and complete with landmarks, a legend, and other map features, that another team will use to find the mystery location.
2. Students develop a set of written instructions using real-world distances and only the words North, South, East, and West or a combination thereof (e.g., Northeast).

Problem Solving

Each team exchanges its completed Mystery Location Map and Directions sheets with another team. Using the directions and the map, teams complete the Discoveries sheets as they discover the mystery location. Each member should complete a Personal Reflection sheet upon completion of the lesson.

Common Core State Standards Met

- CCSS-Math: 6.RP.A Understand ratio concepts and use ratio reasoning to solve problems.
- CCSS-Math: 7.RP.A Analyze proportional relationships and use them to solve real-world and mathematical problems.

Additional Notes

- We suggest instructing students to use the four basic operations to solve the equations they will develop, such as the one shown on the Introduction to Scale Drawing sheet. For example, students will try to solve an equation like $2x = 10$ intuitively by asking the question, "What number multiplied by 2 yields 10?" This strategy will work as long as the problem to be solved is very simple. Consider having students ask the question, "How do I use one of the four basic operations (addition, subtraction, multiplication, or division) to get the variable alone on one side of the equation?" In this case, the answer to that question will be "divide by 2." This is a much more powerful strategy, as it will work to solve equations of greater complexity.

- Students can create their own symbols for lakes, rivers, railroad tracks, and other physical features they may wish to include on their maps as long as they are clearly reported on the legends they develop. All maps should include a legend.
- All teams have the same starting point: their classroom. Ideally, teachers will be able to allow the students to make this a concrete exercise by sending them out to follow the maps to the mystery locations, which would be places within the school or on school grounds. If this is not possible, modify the lesson to have student groups lead each other from their city to another location, following the map and directions on paper only.

Introduction to Scale Drawing

The concept of scale is used to allow cartographers (mapmakers) to show very large areas on a piece of paper.

Example:

How many miles does this line represent?

|————————————————————|

scale: ½ inch = 1 mile

Step 1: Measure the line shown above. How long is it?
Answer: 2 inches.

Step 2: The scale the line is drawn to is ½ inch = 1 mile. That means that ½ inch on paper represents 1 mile in real life.

Step 3: Establish a proportion to discover the length that the line represents in real life using the model: $\frac{a}{b} = \frac{c}{d}$.

$$\frac{\text{½ inch on paper}}{\text{1 mile in real life}} = \frac{\text{2 inches on paper}}{\text{x inches in real life}}$$

The proportion shown above is read, "If ½ inch on paper is 1 mile in real life, then 2 inches on paper equals how many miles in real life?"

Step 4: Solve the proportions by cross-multiplying

$$\frac{1}{2}(x) = 2(1)$$

and isolating the variable (x) on one side of the equation by multiplying

$$\frac{2}{1}\left(\frac{1}{2}x\right) = \frac{2}{1}\left(2(1)\right)$$

$$x = 4$$

Therefore, the 2-inch line shown above represents 4 miles in real life.

Now try the problems on the Scale Drawing Practice sheet!

Math Road Trip © Taylor & Francis Group

Name: _____

Date: _____

Scale Drawing Practice

Measure the distances between the points (A and B) in each exercise to the nearest ¹⁄₁₆ inch. Use the scale that is given with each to determine the length that each line represents in real life.

1. A •——————• B

scale: 1 inch = 20 feet

Answer: _____

2. A •——————————• B

scale: ½ inch = 2 miles

Answer: _____

3. A •————• B

scale: 1 inch = 20 miles

Answer: _____

4. A •——————————• B

scale: 2 inches = 5 feet

Answer: _____

5. A •————————————————• B

scale: ¼ inch = 10 miles

Answer: _____

6. A •————————————————• B

scale: ¼ inch = 1 foot

Answer: _____

7. A •————————• B

scale: ¼ inch = 1 mile

Answer: _____

8. A •——————————• B

scale: ¾ inch = 2 miles

Answer: _____

9. A •————————————————• B

scale: 1 inch = 40 feet

Answer: _____

10. A •————————————————————• B

scale: 1 inch = 25 miles

Answer: _____

Scale Drawing Practice

Answer Key

1. 20 feet
2. 5 miles
3. 15 miles
4. 3.125 feet
5. 90 miles
6. 9 feet
7. 3 miles
8. 3.3 miles
9. 90 feet
10. 43.75 miles

Team: _____

Leader: _____

Navigator: _____

Cartographer: _____

Mystery Location Map

Legend

Scale

Team: _____   Leader: _____

Navigator: _____   Cartographer: _____

Directions

· ·

If you want to find our location . . .

_____

_____

_____

_____

_____

_____

_____

_____

_____

_____

_____

_____

_____

_____

_____

_____

_____

_____

_____

_____

_____

Math Road Trip © Taylor & Francis Group

Team: _____   Leader: _____

Navigator: _____   Cartographer: _____

Discoveries

· ·

1. Where on the map did your journey begin? How did you know where to start?

_____

_____

_____

2. Verification of map information:

Directions	Length of line	Scale	Correct Directions
Example: Starting at point A, go 20 miles NE	2 inches	½ inch = 5 miles	Yes/No
Leg 1			
Leg 2			
Leg 3			
Leg 4			

3. Make a list of directions that were correct. Give evidence.

Correct Directions	Evidence

4. Make a list of directions that were incorrect. Give evidence.

Incorrect Directions	Evidence

Math Road Trip © Taylor & Francis Group
Permission is granted to photocopy or reproduce this page for single classroom use only.

Name:_____ Date: _____

Team: _____

Personal Reflection

What did you like most about this lesson?

_____

_____

What did you like the least?

_____

_____

What would you change to make it more interesting?

_____

_____

Was it more fun to create the map or to follow someone else's map? Why?

_____

_____

How well did your group work together through Lesson 4? Were there any specific problems?

_____

_____

Please make any other comments that would be helpful.

_____

_____

Lesson 5

Concepts

- Teamwork
- The importance of a plan

Materials

- Planning the Ultimate Vacation: Group Expectations sheet (p. 56)
- Planning the Ultimate Vacation: Group Roles sheet (p. 57)
- Planning the Ultimate Vacation: Project Outline sheet (p. 58)
- Planning the Ultimate Vacation: Brainstorm sheet (p. 59)
- The Ultimate Vacation Rating Rubric (p. 60)

Student Objective

Students demonstrate the ability to reach consensus by developing a plan and a list of all of the materials necessary to create the ultimate vacation.

Introduction

This lesson is designed to lay a foundation that will enable students to work collaboratively to successfully complete the requirements of the assigned prompt. At the teacher's discretion, team assignments can be changed to increase productivity. The team assignments made during this lesson will be those that remain throughout the remainder of the unit.

DOI: 10.4324/9781003236511-5

Recognition

Students read and sign the Planning the Ultimate Vacation: Group Expectations sheet.

Application

Students complete the Planning the Ultimate Vacation: Brainstorm sheet.

Problem Solving

Students develop a list of materials needed to complete the assignment (e.g., Internet access, maps) and submit that list to the teacher.

Common Core State Standards Met

Synthesizes core standards met in Lessons 1–4.

Additional Notes

- Lessons 1–4 were designed to prepare students for the book's final activity: planning the ultimate vacation. This is the last opportunity to make any changes to accomplish better group dynamics and/or improve skill matches. We suggest making these assignments collaboratively with students. It's a good time to meet with students to provide information that will make clear their progress or lack thereof thus far in the unit. The positions defined in the Planning the Ultimate Vacation: Group Roles sheet provided in Lesson 1 have been reprised here, and should be used again for this project.
- Please take the time necessary to ensure that each student understands clearly the information contained on The Ultimate Vacation Rating Rubric, and remind them that this instrument will be used in judging their level of success.
- We suggest using this lesson to set the tone for the remainder of their efforts.

Lesson 5

Planning the Ultimate Vacation
Group Expectations

All groups are expected to behave in the following manner:
- Honor each teammate's ideas and work.
- Use constructive criticism when discussing group ideas and work.
- Include all team members in the process.
- Be courteous and civil to each other at all times.
- Attempt to solve conflicts internally.
- Ask the teacher to mediate conflict if necessary.
- Resolve conflict to complete group work.
- Focus on the task at hand and not bring outside conflicts into the project.
- Everyone within the group is expected to pull their own weight to ensure the success of their project.

_____

Name

_____

Name

_____

Name

Math Road Trip © Taylor & Francis Group

Planning the Ultimate Vacation

Group Roles

In this lesson you will need the following roles within your group. Please read the job descriptions carefully and make your recommendations based on team members' strengths. The teacher will make the final assignments.

- **Leader:** This person must be a good negotiator and must be focused and able to encourage others in a positive way. This person is responsible for keeping costs within the budget. The leader is also responsible for providing updates to the teacher when asked. Ultimately, it is the leader's responsibility that the group is successful.
- **Navigator:** This person needs to follow directions, have an attention for detail, and be able to listen to others' suggestions. The navigator is responsible for reading maps and for developing a legend of local landmarks, rivers, lakes, rail lines, and other features when the team creates maps of its own.
- **Cartographer:** The cartographer's job is to create a map of the route that needs to be taken to achieve the group's goal. The map will include landmarks from the legend developed by the navigator.

Leader: _____

Navigator: _____

Cartographer: _____

Please note that this is a group project; therefore, everyone can help in any area, but it is the responsibility of each individual to see that his or her job is complete.

PROJECT OUTLINE

In the course of this project you will be asked to design a vacation for a hypothetical family that lives in another part of the country. You will be given a family profile with important information about your clients. Your team must work to satisfy your clients' needs and not your own interests!

You will be expected to provide driving directions and an original map to help your clients arrive at their destination(s). You are no longer restricted to using only North, South, East, and West in your directions; you may use actual route numbers, street names, and other geographical features. In addition, you will need to provide recommendations for hotels, restaurants, and entertainment. Of course, all of these things come at a price. You must make sure that the proposed plan does not exceed the clients' budget!

After you have completed your plan, including directions, itinerary, and budget sheet, you will need to make a presentation of your plan to your clients. Everything hangs on this presentation—it must be clear and exciting!

Good Luck!

Planning the Ultimate Vacation

Brainstorm

As a group, discuss the things you will need to do to reach your goal. Read the outline and the rubric carefully and highlight the components that are mentioned. List these things below.

Directions to destination:

_____

_____

_____

_____

_____

_____

What steps must you take to be able to accomplish the items on your list? For example, to determine your destination, you must locate your clients' hometown on the map, and then draw a radius of the maximum number of miles they can travel from their home.

_____

_____

_____

_____

_____

_____

The Ultimate Vacation Rating Rubric

	Still in Training	Travel Agent	World Class Planner
Budget	Little or no evidence of logic is applied to the analysis and development of your budget. Mathematical calculations and/or estimations are incorrect.	You use logic to analyze and solve budget problems. Appropriate mathematical strategies are chosen.	Budget problems are analyzed and solved using logic. Appropriate mathematical strategies are chosen that enable you to accurately calculate or estimate needed figures. The travel budget is not only consistent, but it also allows room for unexpected or emergency needs.
Planning	Your planning contains little or no structure. The travel plans fail to follow a logical sequence. You do not consider important aspects of the trip in your plan. Your recommendations for sightseeing and/or other activities are not appropriate for a family vacation.	Your planning is structured. The travel plans follow a logical sequence. You provide sound advice for major aspects of the trip. Recommendations are appropriate, although they tend to favor either the adult or child perspective.	Your planning is well structured and easy to follow. The travel plans are complete and logical. Your advice to the family is unique and inspired. Recommendations are highly appropriate for all family members, offering a good balance between activities that are likely to please adults and those that will please children.
Documents	Overall presentation is messy and hard to understand. Your map is not drawn to scale and does not include important elements. Travel routes are not clearly labeled and mileage is missing. Accompanying materials such as charts and/or graphs are illegible or not clearly related to the itinerary.	Overall presentation is neat and easy to understand. Your map is drawn to scale and includes major elements. Travel routes are labeled, but hard to locate. Mileage is indicated, but in an inconsistent manner. Accompanying materials such as charts and/or graphs are easy to read and relate to the itinerary.	Overall presentation is neat and exciting. Your map is drawn to scale and includes all appropriate elements. Travel routes are clearly labeled and mileage is indicated. Accompanying materials such as charts and/or graphs are professional looking and greatly enhance and/or explain the itinerary.
Mechanics	Information is haphazardly organized. Sentences are not supported by details. Word usage is repetitive, rather than varied. Errors in spelling, punctuation, and grammar make the itinerary difficult to read.	Information is organized. Sentences are supported by details and use a variety of words and phrases. Minor errors in spelling, punctuation, and grammar do not interfere with the message.	Information is clearly and succinctly organized. Each sentence is supported by rich and coherent relevant details. Sentences are highly descriptive and make use of a wide variety of words and phrases. Spelling, punctuation, and grammar are correct.

Lesson 6

Concepts

- Eye contact
- Enunciation
- Projection
- Planning and organizing
- Self-evaluation

Materials

- Planning the Ultimate Vacation: Jobs sheet (p. 64)
- Planning the Ultimate Vacation: Prompts 1–3 (pp. 65–68)
- Planning the Ultimate Vacation: Expense Log sheet (p. 70)
- Family Profiles 1–8 (pp. 72–79)
- Road maps (not provided)
- Tour guidebooks
- AAA Travel Guides

Student Objective

Students demonstrate the ability to plan an ultimate vacation package that has been produced for a hypothetical family by making a presentation to the class.

Introduction

Each team of three students will have 2 days to plan an ultimate vacation experience. Day 3 of this lesson is dedicated to a presentation of the students' vacation proposals.

DOI: 10.4324/9781003236511-6

Recognition

Students show an understanding of the prompt they have been assigned through a group discussion and submission of the Planning the Ultimate Vacation: Jobs sheet.

Application

Students plan and budget the ultimate vacation.

Problem Solving

1. Students present and defend their vacation proposal to the hypothetical family played by their classmates.
2. Students observing the presentations play the role of the family for whom the vacation was planned and participate in completing The Ultimate Vacation Rating Rubric (see Lesson 5) on each presentation.

Common Core State Standards Met

Synthesizes core standards met in Lessons 1–4.

Additional Notes

- Three prompts are provided for your convenience. They are written at slightly varying levels of challenge. Prompt 1 is designed for groups in need of more guidance, while Prompt 3 is intended for students who work more independently. Please choose the one that you feel is most appropriate for each of the groups planning a vacation. The end result is the same and each group should generate similar information for their client regardless of which prompt is chosen.
- You may choose to use the costs associated with rooms and meals provided in Lesson 2, or, now that your students are experienced travelers, you may ask them to provide actual costs based on their research.
- Feel free to adjust the budgets of client families to meet your needs.
- The class plays the role of each client family as they listen to the presentations and are encouraged to ask questions, comment on the appropriateness of recommendations, and make suggestions for improvements.
- At the end of each presentation, allow enough time for each member of the audience (class) to complete The Ultimate Vacation Rating Rubric from Lesson 5 on the presenters and submit it to the teacher.

- Family Profile 8 is provided for your convenience in the event that you wish to customize a family to better suit the needs of your students.
- As the teacher, please feel free to assign family identities to particular groups, or you may simply distribute them randomly.

Name:_____ Date: _____

Planning the Ultimate Vacation
Jobs

At this point, you may be wondering how you will ever get all of the requirements of this project finished. The only possible solution is to divide up the work among the members of your group. You must depend on each other to accomplish this task. It is important that everyone has a clear idea about what their roles are so as not to waste time and energy. Look below at some suggested roles to be filled. There may be others that you come up with as well. You may take on more than one job. (Note that these jobs are to be taken on in addition to the primary roles of leader, navigator, and cartographer.) Please fill in the lines at the bottom of the page and submit the completed form to your teacher.

Leader	Negotiator
	Scheduler
Navigator	Museum expert
	Sports expert
Cartographer	Hiking guide
	Children's entertainment expert
	Restaurant critic
	Hotel expert
	Accountant

Name: _____

Role(s): _____

Name: _____

Role(s): _____

Name: _____

Role(s): _____

Planning the Ultimate Vacation

Prompt 1

The AAA Travel Agency in your town is extremely short-handed and needs additional staff to help travelers plan their vacations. Your task will be to plan a road trip for a family of four (two adults and two children) who want to visit an interesting destination for their vacation. Each family has their own interests that must be met during the trip. None of the families want to travel for more than 2 days to get to their destination because they only have 1 week of vacation time. They average 60 miles per hour and will not drive more than 5 hours per day; therefore, they are limited to a maximum of 600 miles each way. Each family has saved a certain amount for their vacation and you must stay within that budget. You will have access to tour guides and maps to do your work. Use the Expense Log to help you do the following:

1. Calculate the mileage on available routes from your family's hometown to their destination. Remember, the family prefers the shortest route possible.
2. Calculate the approximate cost of gas for the trip. (Assume their car gets 30 mpg and gas costs an average of $3.60 per gallon.)
3. Determine how many nights they will need to spend in hotels on the way to and from their destination. If they stay four nights at their destination, what will be their total cost for hotels?
4. Calculate total meal cost for the trip. The family will eat three meals a day. Budget $75 per day. If your family is to stay in a hotel that offers a complimentary breakfast, deduct $10 per day for the days spent there.
5. Determine recommendations for what to do once the family reaches their destination. The family's entertainment budget is approximately $100 per day. Make suggestions on the best way to spend this money. Be sure to balance the entertainment and activity needs of both the adults and children in the family.
6. Total the cost of travel to the destination and the cost of the trip back home. (If you wish, you may plan an alternate route for their return trip.)
7. Determine if you are within your budget. If not, make whatever changes and/or recommendations you need to be within budget.

You must now prepare a presentation for the family including the following:
*   a detailed itinerary that includes options for travel and recommendations,
*   a proposed budget,
*   a map including travel to, from, and around the destination area,
*   a set of written directions for all travel, and
*   an itemized estimate and detailed explanation of any additional expenses.

You will be evaluated on your ability to advise the family appropriately, the quality of the maps and itinerary you prepare, and the accuracy of your budget.

Planning the Ultimate Vacation

Prompt 2

The AAA Travel Agency in your town is extremely short-handed and needs additional staff to help travelers plan their vacations for next summer. Your task will be to plan a road trip for a family of four (two adults and two children) who want to visit an interesting destination for their vacation next summer. Each family has their own interests that must be met during the trip. None of the families want to travel for more than 2 days to get to their destination because they only have a week of vacation time. They average 60 miles an hour while driving and will not drive more than 5 hours a day; therefore, they are limited to a maximum of 600 miles each way. Each family has saved a certain amount of money for their vacation and you must stay within that amount. You will have access to tour guides and maps to do your work. Use the Expense Log to help you do the following:

1. Calculate the mileage on available routes from your family's hometown to their destination. Remember, the family prefers the shortest route possible.
2. Calculate the approximate cost of gas for the trip. (Assume their car gets 30 mpg and gas costs an average of $3.60 per gallon.)
3. Determine how many nights they will need to spend in hotels on the way to and from their destination. If they stay four nights at their destination, what will be their total cost for hotels?
4. Calculate the total meal cost for the trip. The family will eat three meals a day. Make a recommendation about how much, on average, to budget for each meal. Justify your decision. You may recommend that your family stay in a hotel that offers a complimentary breakfast.
5. Determine recommendations for what to do once the family reaches their destination. The family's entertainment budget is approximately $100 per day. Make recommendations on the best way to spend this money. Be sure to balance the entertainment and activity needs of both the adults and children in the family.
6. Total the cost of travel to the destination and the cost of the trip back home. (If you wish, you may plan an alternate route for their return trip.)
7. Determine if you are within your budget. If not, make whatever changes and/or recommendations you need to be within budget.

You must now prepare a presentation for the family including the following:
- a detailed itinerary that includes options for travel and recommendations,
- a proposed budget,
- a map including travel to, from, and around the destination area,

- a set of written directions for all travel, and
- an itemized estimate and a detailed explanation of additional expenses that the family may incur in order to help them understand the total cost of the vacation.

You will be evaluated on your ability to advise the family appropriately, the quality of the maps and itinerary you prepare, and the accuracy of your budget.

Planning the Ultimate Vacation

Prompt 3

The AAA Travel Agency in your town is extremely short-handed and needs additional staff to help travelers plan their vacations for next summer. Your task will be to plan a road trip for a family of four (two adults and two children) who want to visit an interesting destination for their vacation next summer. Each family has their own interests that must be met during the trip. None of the families want to travel for more than 2 days to get to their destination because they only have a week of vacation time. They average 60 miles an hour and will not drive more than 5 hours a day; therefore, they are limited to a maximum of 600 miles each way. Each family has saved a certain amount of money for their vacation and you must stay within that amount. You will have access to tour guides and maps to do your work. Create a graphic organizer to help you do the following:

1. Calculate the mileage on available routes from your family's hometown to their destination. Remember, the family prefers the shortest route possible.
2. Calculate the approximate cost of gas for the trip. (Assume their car gets 30 mpg and gas costs an average of $3.60 per gallon.)
3. Determine the hotel accommodations expense. How many nights will they need to spend in hotels on the way to and from their destination? If they stay four nights at their destination, what will be their total cost for hotels? (Assume that the family will stay in one room.) Check AAA guidebooks for a hotel with at least a two-diamond rating. The family prefers hotels that provide a complimentary breakfast.
4. Calculate total meal cost for the trip. The family will eat 3 meals a day. Make a recommendation about how much, on average, to budget for each meal. Justify your decision. This family generally eats at fast-food or family-style restaurants, but they like to splurge on one fancy dinner per trip. You will need to make a recommendation on when and where to enjoy this dinner. Also allow for it in the budget.
5. Determine recommendations for what to do once the family reaches their destination. The family's entertainment budget is approximately $100 per day. Make recommendations on the best way to spend this money. Be sure to balance the entertainment and activity needs of both the adults and children in the family.
6. Total the cost of travel to the destination and the cost of the trip back home. They prefer to return home by a different route for variety.

7. Suggest at least one day trip. (The family must be able to drive to the destination, see what they want to see, and return to the hotel in the evening.) Plan a trip that is likely to be interesting for children and adults alike.

8. Determine if you are within your budget. If not, make whatever changes and/or recommendations you need to be within budget.

You must now prepare a presentation for the family including the following:
- a detailed itinerary that includes options for travel and recommendations,
- a proposed budget,
- a map including travel to, from, and around the destination area,
- a set of written directions for all travel, and
- an itemized estimate and detailed explanation of additional expenses that the family may incur in order to help them understand the total cost of the trip.

You will be evaluated on your ability to advise the family appropriately, the quality of the maps and itinerary you prepare, and the accuracy of your budget.

Name:_____ Date: _____

Planning The Ultimate Vacation

Expense Log

Destination: _____ **Budget:**_____

1. Mileage

Route 1: _____ miles

Route 2: _____ miles

Route 3: _____ miles

Use the most direct route to calculate the following items:

2. Cost of Gas

One way = _____ miles

× 2 (round trip) = _____ miles

/ 30 mpg = _____ gallons

× $3.60/gal = _____ total cost of gas*

3. Travel Time

One way = _____ miles

at 60 miles per hour = _____ hours

at 5 hours per day = _____ total days to destination

4. Cost of Hotel

Days of travel = _____ days

× _____ per night = _____ total cost of hotels*

5. Cost of Meals

Total days away from home = _____ days

× _____ food budget per day = _____ total cost of meals*

(*Note:* Remember that your food budget will be cheaper if you stay at hotels that offer complimentary breakfasts!)

6. Cost of Entertainment

Total days at destination = _____ days

× _____ entertainment budget per day

= _____ total entertainment*

* Add to find **Total Cost of Trip:**_____

Math Road Trip © Taylor & Francis Group

71

Permission is granted to photocopy or reproduce this page for single classroom use only.

Family Profile 1

Name: The Boden Family
Dates of Vacation: July 27–Aug. 3, _____
Address: 647 Smith Drive, Santa Barbara, CA

Personal:

Mr. Boden: He is a computer programmer who likes to hike and is a baseball fan.
Mrs. Boden: She is a teacher who likes to shop and go to museums.
Suzie Boden: She is 8 years old, plays soccer and baseball, and loves horses.
Joey Boden: He is 6 years old and loves baseball, football, and science museums.

Interests: This family likes Italian food, swimming, and going to new places.

Special Needs: They have to be back by Aug. 4 so that the kids can try out for soccer teams.

Budget: This family has budgeted $2,400 for their vacation.

Family Profile 2

Name: The Long Family
Dates of Vacation: June 22–30, _____
Address: 345 Canyon Road, Wichita Falls, TX

Personal:

Mr. Long: He is an electrical contractor who likes movies and golf.

Mrs. Long: She is a nurse who likes hiking and listening to music.

Charlie Long: He is 10 years old and likes art and soccer.

Annie Long: She is 3 years old and is very active; she constantly needs to be entertained.

Interests: This family enjoys spending time together, eating in restaurants, and being outdoors.

Special Needs: Annie needs to take a nap in the afternoon and has a strict bedtime of 9 p.m.

Budget: This family has budgeted $2,000 for their vacation.

Family Profile 3

Name: The Alvarez Family
Dates of Vacation: June 1–9, _____
Address: 4839 Union St, Manchester, NH

Personal:

Mr. Alvarez: He is an accountant who likes music and reading.
Mrs. Alvarez: She is a lawyer who likes golf and museums.
Luisa Alvarez: She is 15 years old and likes shopping and art.
Selena Alvarez: She is 12 years old and likes shopping and music.

Interests: Although this is a sophisticated family who are used to living in a big city, they would like to explore the outdoors more. They want to try things they have never done before.

Special Needs: None.

Budget: This family has budgeted $2,500 for their vacation.

Family Profile 4

Name: The Hunt Family
Dates of Vacation: June 30–July 7, _____
Address: 478 Cherry Tree Lane, Trenton, NJ

Personal:

Mr. Hunt: He is a colonel in the U.S. Air Force. He likes exploring new places and relaxing by the pool.
Mrs. Hunt: She is a teacher who likes reading and hiking.
Laura Hunt: She is 8 years old and likes swimming and movies.
Jonathan Hunt: He is 6 years old and likes video games and active sports.

Interests: This family enjoys historical places and a variety of activities.

Special Needs: This family sunburns easily. It is better for them to be out of the sun during the peak hours of 11 a.m.–3 p.m.

Budget: This family has budgeted $2,300 for their vacation.

Math Road Trip © Taylor & Francis Group

75

Permission is granted to photocopy or reproduce this page for single classroom use only.

Family Profile 5

Name: The O'Hara Family
Dates of Vacation: August 4–11, _____
Address: 46 Smith Road, Atlanta, GA

Personal:
Mr. O'Hara: He is a retired banker who likes to golf and enjoys boating.
Mrs. O'Hara: She is a retired music teacher who loves music and arts and crafts.
Steve O'Hara: He is their 13-year-old grandson. He likes history and computers.
Peter O'Hara: He is their 11-year-old grandson. He likes all sports and video games.

Interests: These grandparents are taking their grandchildren on a vacation for the first time. They want to expose the boys to new experiences and want them to have fun.

Special Needs: Mr. O'Hara has a heart condition and needs to rest in the afternoons.

Budget: This family has budgeted $3,000 for a vacation.

Family Profile 6

Name: The Smith-James Family
Dates of Vacation: August 11–18, _____
Address: 64 Humboldt Rd., Tampa, FL

Personal:

Dr. James: He is a surgeon who likes to skydive and rock climb.

Dr. Smith-James: She is an obstetrician who likes hiking and going to the theater.

Mallory Smith-James: She is 17 years old and likes swimming, dancing, and shopping.

Eddie Smith-James: He is 14 years old and likes music, video games, and sports.

Interests: This family loves being outdoors and enjoys physically active pursuits.

Special Needs: Both parents need Internet access to check messages and contact their offices for emergencies.

Budget: This family has budgeted $3,500 for their vacation.

Family Profile 7

Name: The Brown Family
Dates of Vacation: Variable
Address: 893 Rattle Snake Canyon Rd., Tucson, AZ

Personal:
Mr. Brown: He is an author who likes to take long hikes and visit museums.
Mrs. Brown: She is a business executive who loves history and art.
Julie Brown: She is 4 years old and loves music and swimming.
Elias Brown: He is 2 years old and is an active toddler.

Interests: This family likes to explore new places.

Special Needs: The children wake early and need lots of activity in the morning as well as an afternoon nap. They need to be in bed by 9 p.m.

Budget: This family has budgeted $2,200 for their vacation.

Family Profile 8

Name: _____

Dates of Vacation: _____

Address: _____

Personal:

_____

_____

_____

Interests: _____

_____

Special Needs: _____

_____

Budget: _____

Lesson 7

Concepts

- Self-evaluation
- Unit evaluation

Materials

- Evaluation sheet (p. 82)
- Math Skills Delineator (see Lesson 1)

Student Objective

Students evaluate the quality of the *Math Road Trip* unit and their performance while engaged in the unit by completing the Evaluation sheet and the Math Skills Delineator as a posttest.

Introduction

The teacher leads a discussion of the benefits of self-evaluation and the importance of accepting constructive criticism.

Recognition

Students respond to teacher questions to document an understanding of the importance of self-evaluation, accepting constructive criticism, and content understanding.

DOI: 10.4324/9781003236511-7

Application

Students complete the Evaluation sheet.

Problem Solving

1. Students suggest changes they would make to improve the unit.
2. Students complete the Math Skills Delineator.

Common Core State Standards Met

Synthesizes core standards met in Lessons 1–4.

Additional Notes

- Recognizing what has been learned is a skill very few middle school students possess. When asked "What did you learn at school today?", the most common answer heard is "nothing." We suggest that you lead a discussion and create at the board (or on another device) a list that students will generate of what they have learned. Two fields of information will be brought forward as part of such a discussion. One will be content related—for example, a strategy to solve basic equations or a better understanding of scale drawing. The other area that we sense students will recognize will be from the implicit curriculum we all work at teaching—for example, patience when working with others or the importance of teamwork to accomplish a goal.

Evaluation

Name: _____

Team: _____

Destination: _____

1. Please check the parts of your project that you found most challenging:
    - ❏ Staying within budget
    - ❏ Drawing to scale
    - ❏ Working with fractions

2. Which of the following statements describe your team? Check all that apply:
    - ❏ Maintained focus
    - ❏ Worked well together
    - ❏ Were able to talk out differences
    - ❏ Were able to agree when making decisions
    - ❏ Were able to benefit from constructive criticism

3. Was adequate time provided to prepare the trip?
    - ❏ Yes
    - ❏ No

4. Our team:
    - ❏ Used time well, easily making all deadlines
    - ❏ Started out well, but became distracted and lost track of time
    - ❏ Thought it was helpful to have time reminders

5. Please evaluate the following roles as they apply to your team.
    - The Leader was:
        - ❏ Focused and stayed on task
        - ❏ Had a difficult time with the necessary computations
        - ❏ Easily mastered the skills necessary for the job
        - ❏ Was cooperative and helpful to others

    - The Navigator was:
        - ❏ Focused and stayed on task
        - ❏ Had a difficult time with the necessary computations
        - ❏ Easily mastered the skills necessary for the job
        - ❏ Was cooperative and helpful to others

- The Cartographer was:
  - ❏ Focused and stayed on task
  - ❏ Had a difficult time with the necessary computations
  - ❏ Easily mastered the skills necessary for the job
  - ❏ Was cooperative and helpful to others

6. Maps are:
  - ❏ Something I use often
  - ❏ Something I was completely unfamiliar with until this unit
  - ❏ Interesting and useful
  - ❏ Very difficult to read

7. I liked/disliked my role because:

_____

_____

8. I would have preferred to be a:
- Navigator
- Leader
- Cartographer

Please explain why.

_____

_____

9. Please reflect on the unit. Be sure to include the part you liked best and the part you liked least. What is one thing you would change to make the unit better?

_____

_____

Appendix
Student Context
Rubric

The Student Context Rubric (SCR) is intended for use by the classroom teacher as a tool to help in the identification of students of masked potential. This term, *masked potential*, refers to students who are gifted, but are frequently not identified because their behaviors are not displayed to best advantage by traditional methods. The SCR was designed to be used with this series of units and the authentic performance assessments that accompany them. Although you may choose to run the units without using the SCR, you may find the rubric helpful for keeping records of student behaviors.

The units serve as platforms for the display of student behaviors, while the SCR is an instrument that teachers can use to record those behaviors when making observations. The rubric requires the observer to record the frequency of gifted behaviors, but there is also the option to note that the student demonstrates the behavior with particular intensity. In this way, the rubric is subjective and requires careful observation and consideration.

It is recommended that an SCR be completed for each student prior to the application of a unit, and once again upon completion of the unit. In this way, teachers will be reminded of behaviors to look for during the unit—particularly those behaviors that we call *loophole behaviors*, which may indicate giftedness but are often misinterpreted or overlooked. (For instance, a student's verbal ability can be missed if he or she uses it to spin wild lies about having neglected to complete an assignment.) Therefore, the SCR allows teachers to be aware of—and to document—high-ability behavior even if it is masked or used in nontraditional ways. The mechanism also provides a method for tracking changes in teachers' perceptions of their students, not only while students are working on the Interactive Discovery-Based Units for High-Ability Learners, but also while they are engaged in traditional classroom activities.

In observing student behaviors, you might consider some of the following questions after completing a lesson:

- Was there anyone or anything that surprised you today?
- Did a particular student jump out at you today?
- Did someone come up with a unique or unusual idea today?
- Was there a moment in class today when you saw a lightbulb go on? Did it involve an individual, a small group, or the class as a whole?
- In reviewing written responses after a class discussion, were you surprised by anyone (either because he or she was quiet during the discussion but had good written ideas, or because he or she was passionate in the discussion but did not write with the same passion)?
- Did any interpersonal issues affect the classroom today? If so, how were these issues resolved?
- Did the lesson go as planned today? Were there any detours?
- Is there a student whom you find yourself thinking or worrying about outside of school?
- Are there students in your classroom who seem to be on a rollercoaster of learning—"on" one day, but "off" the next?
- Are your students different outside of the classroom? In what ways are they different?
- Are there students who refuse to engage with the project?
- During a class performance, did the leadership of a group change when students got in front of their peers?
- Did your students generate new ideas today?
- What was the energy like in your class today? Did you provide the energy, or did the students?
- How long did it take the students to engage today?

Ideally, multiple observers complete the SCR for each student. If a gifted and talented specialist is available, we recommend that he or she assist. By checking off the appropriate marks to describe student behaviors, and by completing the scoring chart, participants generate quantifiable data that can be used in advocating for students who would benefit from scaffolded services. **In terms of students' scores on the SCR, we do not provide concrete cutoffs or point requirements regarding which students should be recommended for special services.** Rather, the SCR is intended to flag students for scaffolded services and to enable them to reach their potential. It also provides a way to monitor and record students' behaviors.

What follows is an explanation of the categories and items included on the SCR, along with some examples of how the specified student behaviors might be evidenced in your classroom.

Engagement

1. **Student arrives in class with new ideas to bring to the project that he or she has thought of outside of class.** New ideas may manifest themselves as ideas about how to approach a problem, about new research information found on the Internet or elsewhere outside of class, about something in the news or in the paper that is relevant to the subject, or about a connection between the subject and an observed behavior.

2. **Student shares ideas with a small group of peers, but may fade into the background in front of a larger group.** The student may rise to be a leader when the small group is working on a project, but if asked to get up in front of the class, then that student fades into the background and lets others do the talking.

3. **Student engagement results in a marked increase in the quality of his or her performance.** This is particularly evident in a student who does not normally engage in class at all. During the unit, the student suddenly becomes engaged and produces something amazing.

4. **Student eagerly interacts with appropriate questions, but may be reluctant to put things down on paper.** This is an example of a loophole behavior, or one that causes a student to be overlooked when teachers and specialists are identifying giftedness. It is particularly evident in students who live in largely "oral" worlds, which is to say that they communicate best verbally and are often frustrated by written methods, or in those who have writing disabilities.

Creativity

1. **Student intuitively makes "leaps" in his or her thinking.** Occasionally, you will be explaining something, and a lightbulb will go on for a student, causing him or her to take the concept far beyond the content being covered. Although there are students who do this with regularity, it is more often an intensity behavior, meaning that when it occurs, the student is very intense in his or her thinking, creativity, reasoning, and so on. This can be tricky to identify, because often, the student is unable to explain his or her thinking, and the teacher realizes only later that a leap in understanding was achieved.

2. **Student makes up new rules, words, or protocols to express his or her own ideas.** This can take various forms, one of which is a student's taking

two words and literally combining them to try to express what he or she is thinking about. Other times, a student will want to change the rules to make his or her idea possible.

3. **Student thinks on his or her feet in response to a project challenge, to make excuses, or to extend his or her work.** This is another loophole behavior, because it often occurs when a student is being defensive or even misbehaving, making a teacher less likely to interpret it as evidence of giftedness. It is sometimes on display during classroom debates and discussions.

4. **Student uses pictures or other inventive means to illustrate his or her ideas.** Given the choice, this student would rather draw an idea than put it into words. This could take the shape of the student creating a character web or a design idea. The student might also act out an idea or use objects to demonstrate understanding.

Synthesis

1. **Student goes above and beyond directions to expand ideas.** It is wonderful to behold this behavior in students, particularly when displayed by those students who are rarely engaged. A student may be excited about a given idea and keep generating increasingly creative or complex material to expand upon that idea. For instance, we had a student who, during the mock trial unit, became intrigued by forensic evidence and decided to generate and interpret evidence to bolster his team's case.

2. **Student has strong opinions on projects, but may struggle to accept directions that contradict his or her opinions.** This student may understand directions, but be unwilling to yield to an idea that conflicts with his or her own idea. This behavior, rather than indicating a lack of understanding, is typical of students with strong ideas.

3. **Student is comfortable processing new ideas.** This behavior is evident in students who take new ideas and quickly extend them or ask insightful questions.

4. **Student blends new and old ideas.** This behavior has to do with processing a new idea, retrieving an older idea, and relating the two to one another. For instance, a student who learns about using string to measure distance might remember making a treasure map and extrapolate that a string would have been useful for taking into account curves and winding paths.

Interpersonal Ability

1. **Student is an academic leader who, when engaged, increases his or her levels of investment and enthusiasm in the group.** This is a student who has so much enthusiasm for learning that he or she makes the project engaging for the whole group, fostering an attitude of motivation or optimism.

2. **Student is a social leader in the classroom, but may not be an academic leader.** To observe this type of behavior, you may have to be vigilant, for

some students are disengaged in the classroom but come alive as soon as they cross the threshold into the hallway, where they can socialize with their peers. Often, this student is able to get the rest of the group to do whatever he or she wants (and does not necessarily use this talent for good).

3. **Student works through group conflict to enable the group to complete its work.** When the group has a conflict, this is the student who solves the problem or addresses the issue so that the group can get back to work. This is an interpersonal measure, and thus, it does not describe a student who simply elects to do all of the work rather than confronting his or her peers about sharing the load.

4. **Student is a Tom Sawyer in classroom situations, using his or her charm to get others to do the work.** There is an important distinction to watch out for when identifying this type of behavior: You must be sure that the student is *not* a bully, coercing others to do his or her work. Instead, this student actually makes other students *want* to lend a helping hand. For instance, a twice-exceptional student who is highly talented but struggles with reading might develop charm in order to get other students to transpose his verbally expressed ideas into writing.

Verbal Communication

1. **Participation in brainstorming sessions (e.g., group work) increases student's productivity.** When this type of student is given the opportunity to verbally process with peers, he or she is often able to come up with the answer. For instance, if asked outright for an answer, this student may shrug, but if given a minute to consult with a neighbor, then the student usually is able and willing to offer the correct answer.

2. **Student constructively disagrees with peers and/or the teacher by clearly sharing his or her thoughts.** This student can defend his or her point of view with examples and reasoning—not just in a formal debate, but also in general classroom situations. He or she has learned to channel thoughts into constructive disagreement, rather than flying off the handle merely to win an argument.

3. **Student verbally expresses his or her academic and/or social needs.** This student can speak up when confused or experiencing personality clashes within a group. This student knows when to ask for help and can clearly articulate what help is needed.

4. **Student uses strong word choice and a variety of tones to bring expression to his or her verbal communication.** This student is an engaging speaker and speaks loudly and clearly enough for everybody to hear. A wide vocabulary is also indicative that this student's verbal capability is exceptional.

Student: _____

Date: _____

Fill out the rubric according to what you have observed about each student's behaviors. Then, for each area, record the number of items you marked "Not observed," "Sometimes," and "Often." Multiply these tallies by the corresponding point values (0, 1, and 2) to get the totals for each area. There is an option to check for high intensity so you can better keep track of students' behaviors.

STUDENT CONTEXT RUBRIC

ENGAGEMENT

1. Student arrives in class with new ideas to bring to the project that he or she has thought of outside of class.
   NOT OBSERVED · SOMETIMES · OFTEN · HIGH INTENSITY

2. Student shares ideas with a small group of peers, but may fade into the background in front of a larger group.
   NOT OBSERVED · SOMETIMES · OFTEN · HIGH INTENSITY

3. Student engagement results in a marked increase in the quality of his or her performance.
   NOT OBSERVED · SOMETIMES · OFTEN · HIGH INTENSITY

4. Student eagerly interacts with appropriate questions, but may be reluctant to put things down on paper.
   NOT OBSERVED · SOMETIMES · OFTEN · HIGH INTENSITY

CREATIVITY

1. Student intuitively makes "leaps" in his or her thinking.
   NOT OBSERVED · SOMETIMES · OFTEN · HIGH INTENSITY

2. Student makes up new rules, words, or protocols to express his or her own ideas.
   NOT OBSERVED · SOMETIMES · OFTEN · HIGH INTENSITY

3. Student thinks on his or her feet in response to a project challenge, to make excuses, or to extend his or her work.
   NOT OBSERVED · SOMETIMES · OFTEN · HIGH INTENSITY

4. Student uses pictures or other inventive means to illustrate his or her ideas.
   NOT OBSERVED · SOMETIMES · OFTEN · HIGH INTENSITY

SYNTHESIS

1. Student goes above and beyond directions to expand ideas.
   NOT OBSERVED · SOMETIMES · OFTEN · HIGH INTENSITY

2. Student has strong opinions on projects, but may struggle to accept directions that contradict his or her opinions.
   NOT OBSERVED · SOMETIMES · OFTEN · HIGH INTENSITY

3. Student is comfortable processing new ideas.
   NOT OBSERVED · SOMETIMES · OFTEN · HIGH INTENSITY

4. Student blends new ideas and old ideas.
   NOT OBSERVED · SOMETIMES · OFTEN · HIGH INTENSITY

INTERPERSONAL ABILITY

1. Student is an academic leader who, when engaged, increases his or her levels of investment and enthusiasm in the group.
   NOT OBSERVED · SOMETIMES · OFTEN · HIGH INTENSITY

2. Student is a social leader in the classroom, but may not be an academic leader.
   NOT OBSERVED · SOMETIMES · OFTEN · HIGH INTENSITY

3. Student works through group conflict to enable the group to complete its work.
   NOT OBSERVED · SOMETIMES · OFTEN · HIGH INTENSITY

4. Student is a Tom Sawyer in classroom situations, using his or her charm to get others to do the work.
   NOT OBSERVED · SOMETIMES · OFTEN · HIGH INTENSITY

VERBAL COMMUNICATION

1. Participation in brainstorming sessions (e.g., group work) increases student's productivity.
   NOT OBSERVED · SOMETIMES · OFTEN · HIGH INTENSITY

2. Student constructively disagrees with peers and/or the teacher by clearly sharing his or her thoughts.
   NOT OBSERVED · SOMETIMES · OFTEN · HIGH INTENSITY

3. Student verbally expresses his or her academic and/or social needs.
   NOT OBSERVED · SOMETIMES · OFTEN · HIGH INTENSITY

4. Student uses strong word choice and a variety of tones to bring expression to his or her verbal communication.
   NOT OBSERVED · SOMETIMES · OFTEN · HIGH INTENSITY

AREA	NOT 0	SOME 1	OFTEN 2	HIGH	TOTAL
ENGAGEMENT					
CREATIVITY					
SYNTHESIS					
INTERPERSONAL ABILITY					
VERBAL COMMUNICATION					
ADD TOTALS					

About the Authors

Richard G. Cote, M.B.A., is a career educator. He has dedicated 41 years to being a classroom teacher (mathematics, physics), a community college adjunct instructor (economics), a gifted and talented resource specialist, and the director of the Further Steps Forward Project, a Javits Grant program.

His development of the MESH (mathematics, English, science, and history) program has led him to several audiences. He has presented at various national conventions, civic/community groups, district school boards, teacher organizations, community colleges, and universities, and has served as a consultant to educators throughout the country. Cote helped develop the teacher certification examination for physics at the Institute for Educational Testing and Research at the University of South Florida. He completed the Florida Council on Educational Management Program in Educational Leadership, and he is the recipient of numerous awards, including a certificate of merit on economics education from the University of South Florida, a grant from the Florida Council on Economics Education, a Florida Compact award, and prestigious NAGC Curriculum Studies awards for the development of the Interactive Discovery-Based Units for High-Ability Learners series.

Now retired from the workplace, Cote continues to share his energy, creativity, and expertise with educators through the Interactive Discovery-Based Units for High-Ability Learners.

Darcy O. Blauvelt has been teaching in a variety of facilities for more than 12 years. Her educational journey has included public schools, private schools, nursery schools, and a professional theatre for children ages 3–18. Blauvelt holds educational certification in Theatre K–12, Early Childhood Education, and English Education 5–12. She holds a B.A. in theatre from Chatham College, Pittsburgh, PA, and has done graduate work at Lesley University in Massachusetts in creative arts in learning, as well as at Millersville University in Pennsylvania in psychology.

In 2005, she joined the Nashua School District as a gifted and talented resource specialist. Subsequently, she served full time as the program coordinator for the Further Steps Forward Project, a Javits Grant program, from 2005–2009. Blauvelt returned to the classroom in the fall of 2009 and currently teaches seventh-grade English in Nashua, NH. Blauvelt lives in Manchester, NH, with her husband, two dogs, five cats, and the occasional son!

Common Core State Standards Alignment

Lesson	Common Core State Standards in Math
Lesson 1	6.NS.A Apply and extend previous understandings of multiplication and division to divide fractions by fractions.
	6.NS.C Apply and extend previous understandings of numbers to the system of rational numbers.
	6.RP.A Understand ratio concepts and use ratio reasoning to solve problems.
	7.NS.A Apply and extend previous understandings of operations with fractions.
Lesson 2	6.RP.A Understand ratio concepts and use ratio reasoning to solve problems.
	7.RP.A Analyze proportional relationships and use them to solve real-world and mathematical problems.
Lesson 3	6.RP.A Understand ratio concepts and use ratio reasoning to solve problems.
	6.SP.B Summarize and describe distributions
Lesson 4	6.RP.A Understand ratio concepts and use ratio reasoning to solve problems.
	7.RP.A Analyze proportional relationships and use them to solve real-world and mathematical problems.

Lesson	Common Core State Standards in Math
Lesson 5	Synthesizes all standards listed for Lessons 1-4.
Lesson 6	Synthesizes all standards listed for Lessons 1-4.
Lesson 7	Synthesizes all standards listed for Lessons 1-4.

Key: NS = The Number System; RP = Ratios & Proportional Relationships; SP = Statistics & Probability

For Product Safety Concerns and Information please contact our EU representative GPSR@taylorandfrancis.com Taylor & Francis Verlag GmbH, Kaufingerstraße 24, 80331 München, Germany

Printed and bound by CPI Group (UK) Ltd, Croydon, CR0 4YY

07/07/2025

01912353-0001